CABIN *Style*

Ideas & Projects
for Your World

JERRI FARRIS AND TIM HIMSEL

CREATIVE
PUBLISHING
international

CHANHASSEN, MINNESOTA

www.creativepub.com

CONTENTS

PROJECTS

$\mathcal{P}$REFACE

For several years in the early 90s, I had a cabin on a lake in northern Minnesota. That cabin was my heart's true home, and I loved everything about it. There was no bad weather there. Sunshine found us on the lake, swimming, fishing, skiing, or just playing around on the small armada of water toys that accumulated. Rain brought its own entertainments—a cozy fire and board games, cards, or reading. Movie marathons were always a possibility, too. Friends and family came often and stayed as long as possible.

The cabin was eventually sold, a casualty of divorce. Even so, my relationships with my children have been shaped by time spent at cabins—first our own and then others that we rented or were invited to by friends throughout the years. Evan and Katie learned to build fires, tie knots, and even drive in the northwoods of Minnesota, surrounded by its 10,000 lakes.

The kids are nearly grown now, but every once in a while, the smell of a forest on a rainy day or the sight of sunlight dancing on the water sends my senses reeling. For a moment, I'm back in the days when they were small, and the three of us spent summer weekends in places where life was simple and hot dogs cooked over a bonfire were considered haute cuisine.

Tim, the designer and creative light of *Cabin Style,* grew up on a farm in Wisconsin, in the house where his mother had been born and raised. When he was a young boy, his mom and dad remodeled the kitchen, adding on a family room as well. The centerpiece of the addition—indeed, of the house—was a whole-wall fireplace constructed of stones pulled from the fields of the family farm. Tim says that was his introduction to the atmosphere created by natural, rustic materials. He has fond memories of the way his mother accessorized the fieldstone wall and mantle—a collection of butterchurns at one time, antique crocks at another.

Tim Himsel and Jerri Farris

When Tim and I launched into developing *Cabin Style*, we once again found ourselves at the center of a chaotic, creative whirlwind. John Ruskin once said that harmony happens when love and skill work together.

Developing this book was an absolute delight, and its harmony is a tribute to the skills, talents, and hard work of a wonderful group of people. Tim and I would like to thank everyone involved in the process, especially Paul Gorton, for exercising his talents as an All-American Scrounger; Sheila Duffy for her extraordinary sample making; Randy Austin for his patience as well as his construction skills; Julie Caruso for the grace she brings to the projects and photographs; John Rajtar for his virtuoso propping and styling;

Andrea Rugg and Tate Carlson for their gorgeous photography; and Tracy Stanley and Jon Simpson for keeping the whole shooting match moving forward in a semi-orderly fashion.

Last, but by no means least, we want to thank all the people who shared their cabin memories and stories with us. A special thank you to Nicole Hepokoski, Michelle Kackman, Kristen McCurry Mohn, Michelle Skudlarek, and Ben Olson, whose stories became the heart and soul of *Cabin Style*.

Jerri Farris

ℐNTRODUCTION

From the Atlantic seaboard to the Pacific Northwest, and everywhere in between, people have built and treasured rustic retreats for generations. Maybe it's an idealized image of pioneer days, maybe it's the magnetic pull of childhood memories, but there's no denying that the cabin lifestyle appeals to a large and growing number of people. The construction of log homes in the United States alone is a billion dollar industry these days.

Every spring, here in Minnesota thousands of cabins are opened, aired, and prepared for the all-too-short season. When I first moved here, this phenomenon was a mystery to me. We had plenty of rustic cabins down in the Ozark Mountains where I grew up, but they were people's homes, not weekend retreats. I've since come to understand that the cabin experience is common to much of North America. And most people who grew up visiting cabins have strong emotional ties to those times and places.

When we began to research this book, we talked to many people about their experiences with, and memories of, cabins. We asked what makes cabins different from small houses. We asked what makes cabins so special. And then we sat back and watched as people's faces lit up and their stories poured out.

Certain themes surfaced in story after story and conversation after conversation. When all is said and done, cabins are simple, comfortable dwellings that hold connections to the past and promises for the future. They're places where guests are always welcome and there's always time for fun.

The term *cabin* has been applied to everything from primitive shacks to the grand lodges of the old Adirondack camps. As much as anything else, cabin style is a state of mind, an emotional connection. And it doesn't depend on size or location or structure.

Cabins have certain characteristics in common, however. Whatever else they may be, cabins are:

Rustic   *Relaxing*   *Welcoming*

Simple   *Comfortable*   *Timeless*

By incorporating these same characteristics, you can bring cabin style into your home and your life, no matter where you live.

Cabins typically reflect the natural landscapes that surround them. It may be easy to reflect a mountain, forest, river, or lake that's right outside your door, but what do you do when your home is surrounded by an urban or suburban neighborhood? Not to worry. No matter where you live, you can create an atmosphere that reflects your inner landscape.

The first thing to do is look within and identify the shapes, colors, textures, sights, and sounds that are imprinted on your heart and in your memory. Start by letting your imagination wander through your subconscious for a bit.

Buy a spiral-bound sketch book, 11 × 14" or so. This will be your work-book, and its pages will reveal that inner landscape. If you grew up going to a cabin, spend some time recalling favorite memories. Daydream about those times, and make notes. Jot down descriptive words. If you can draw, sketch your memories.

Next, go through magazines, and cut out pictures of natural landscapes and wilderness settings that appeal to you. Don't try to make the photos match or go together or follow a theme—just gather images that speak to your spirit, and glue them into random collages.

Eventually, patterns will emerge. Textures, colors, or themes will be repeat-ed. These are the characteristics of the landscape of your heart, and they're the elements you should include in your cabin-style rooms. For example, if you choose picture after picture of pine forests, then pine trees and pine cones should find places in your cabin-style decorating. If rivers are a con-stant theme, include river stone in prominent places.

If you spend enough time visiting cabins or looking at photographs of them, you'll find that certain motifs surface in almost every region across North America. These include:

- Wild animals, such as bear, deer, moose, and sometimes elk or buffalo
- Birds, particularly waterfowl and eagles
- Freshwater fish
- Trees, especially birch and pine
- Native American artifacts

There are regional variations, of course. In the western United States and Canada, cowboy regalia and other items related to the Old West are wildly popular. In Maine, blueberries crop up frequently. And Minnesotans are simply crazy about loons. Some variations are related to the history and heritage of an area—buffalo plaids are especially common in places like the Pacific Northwest, where lumberjacks once roamed, for example.

Using any of these motifs will quickly bring a cabin feel into your home. It doesn't matter whether or not you live in the region where they're most common. Just pick the elements that speak to your heart and soul and work them into your decor. Start with rustic treatments for walls, floors, and ceilings, then concentrate on comfortable, durable furnishings that welcome family and friends and are carefree enough to leave you plenty of time to enjoy both. Finally, add accessories inspired by the inner landscape you discovered. Throughout *Cabin Style*, you'll find hundreds of ideas and dozens of projects that can help.

Rustic
is a state of mind.

Like beauty, *rustic* is in the eye of the beholder. The Adirondack camps of the 30s and 40s were considered rustic by the standards of the giants-of-industry, multi-millionaire mogul-types who established them, but most of the rest of us would—then and now— consider them incredibly elegant. The grand scale of the rooms and fur-nishings, and the level of detail and craftsmanship that were put into them exceed anything found in most of today's homes, let alone cabins.

At the other end of the spectrum, North America is filled with small houses in rural areas, but most of them aren't cabins, just average homes in small towns.

So, what is rustic? And how does it contribute to cabin style? Well, the dictionary defines *rustic* as something that is plain, that lacks polish or sophistication, and that's a good place to begin. Rough textures, matte finishes, earth-tone colors, hand-wrought details—all these are compo-nents of the kind of atmosphere that sets the stage for cabin-style rooms.

Throughout the pages of this book, you'll find wonderful photographs of cabins and cabin-style rooms, many of which feature huge beamed ceilings, log walls, and plank floors. Don't be discouraged if your home doesn't include those hallmark architectural features. With some imagination and a little bit of work, you can create a rustic atmosphere without them.

For example, the physical structure of the bedroom at left is pretty much what you'd find in a million standard suburban homes. Even so, the room exudes cabin style. That style results from a series of careful choices—the warm red of the walls, the bold plaid of the window treatments, the Native American rug at the end of the bed, to name a few.

The bedroom above has more elaborate structural details, but they're painted stark white, an inviting background for the rustic furnishings and accessories that give the room its cabin-style ambience. The floor in this room suggests a simple trick that could be used anywhere: arrange overlapping area rugs to hide worn or damaged floors or even disguise wall-to-wall carpeting.

The next few pages illustrate a series of easy, inexpensive ideas that will help you create rustic settings for your cabin-style rooms.

CEILINGS

Wood ceilings infuse a room with rustic character, and can be as elaborate or as simple as your budget and skills allow. For example, rough-cut 2 × 4s were added to a flat ceiling to imitate exposed framing in the family room at right. This is a fairly inexpensive, easy process.

Using an electronic stud finder, locate and mark the beams and joists in the ceiling and the studs in the walls. Use the beams and joists as nailing surfaces to anchor the rough-cut lumber in a grid across the ceiling. At the walls, install 2 × 4s around the room as you would crown molding, nailing them to the wall studs.

The tongue-and-groove paneled ceiling in the bedroom below is more expensive and slightly more time-consuming to install, but the warmth of its presence makes it more than worth the effort. With careful advance planning and the right tools, you could panel an average-sized bedroom ceiling in a weekend. Start by locating the beams, joists, and wall studs. Plan a layout that utilizes the framing as an anchor, starts and ends with boards of equal size, and varies the placement of the joints. Fit the tongues and grooves together, and blindnail the boards in place. Finish with trim nailed to the wall studs.

WALLS

Wainscoting, which typically covers the lower three to four feet (about 1 m) of a wall, is a quick way to provide a rustic background for a cabin-style room. You can paint or stain the boards, depending on the room's furnishings and the ambience you want to create. In the bathroom below, the stained wainscoting blends the wallboard wall into its rugged, timber-lined surroundings. The painted wainscoting in the basement bedroom at right draws attention away from the exposed mechanicals in the ceiling.

Tongue-and-groove wainscoting usually is made of pine, fir, or other soft wood. If you're planning to stain the wainscoting, pick a wood species with a pronounced grain, such as pine. You can stain the wood with oil-based stain, either before or after installation, since most of the stain will be absorbed into the wood and won't interfere with the joints. On the other hand, if you're painting, it's better to use a species with few knots and a consistent grain, such as poplar. Prime and paint the boards after they're installed so the paint doesn't enlarge the tongues or clog the grooves.

WALLS

Textured plaster or adobe-type walls provide an especially appropriate background for cabin-style rooms with a Southwestern flavor. If you don't already have those types of walls, it's easy to imitate them with texture paints.

Texture paints are available in premixed latex formulations or in powder form. The premixed varieties are fine for producing light stipple patterns, but powder textures are a better choice for creating heavier adobe or stucco finishes.

Powder textures must be mixed with water, using a paint mixer bit on a power drill. Practice texturing on cardboard until you get the pattern you want. Remember that the depth of the texture depends on the stiffness of the texture paint, the amount you apply, and the type of tool you use.

Here are some simple suggestions:

• Apply the texture paint with a roller, then use a whisk broom to create a swirl pattern.

• Roll the texture paint onto the walls, brush it out level, then randomly strike the surface with the flat side of the brush to make a crows-foot design.

• Trowel texture paint onto the wall, and pile the material in ridges to make an adobe pattern.

• Roll on the texture paint and let it partially dry. Trowel over the texture to flatten the peaks. Clean the trowel between strokes.

To emphasize the texture, color wash the walls with two closely related neutral colors of paint.

FLOORS

Floors offer yet another opportunity to set a rustic tone for cabin-style rooms. Wide plank wood floors are ideal, either stained or painted, such as the bedroom at left. It might be a shame to paint a hardwood floor in prime condition, but if you have a wood floor that isn't in the best shape, several coats of latex paint can make it a star.

Aged finishes give floors timeworn character and, though they may appear fragile, are actually very durable. These finishes are easiest to produce on previously painted or stained floors. However, they can be applied to new or resurfaced flooring if you apply stain-killing primer over any knotholes and then apply a coat of clear acrylic sealer to keep the paint from penetrating the grain of the wood.

Clean previously painted floors with TSP (trisodium phosphate) to remove any wax, grease, or oil. Rinse the floor with clear water and let it dry. Next, sand the floor in the direction of the wood grain, using fine-grit sandpaper. Vacuum the floor thoroughly, then wipe it with a tack cloth to remove the dust.

Apply two or three coats of latex enamel floor paint, a different color for each coat. Between coats, let the paint dry thoroughly, then lightly sand, using fine-grit sandpaper. Wipe the floor with a tack cloth before applying the next coat.

To reveal the layers of color, sand the floor surface with medium-grit sandpaper, sanding harder in some areas to remove the top and middle coats of paint. Avoid sanding beyond the base coat of paint or stain.

Delight in things
Simple.

My neighbor at the cabin had a clever way of keeping things simple. He made a rule that if something was brought into his cabin, something else had to be taken out. Before he bought anything, he evaluated how much he liked, needed, or wanted it, and considered what he would give up in order to have it. This plan takes some self discipline, but certainly helps reduce clutter.

True cabins are smaller than year-round homes, and often contain fewer amenities. But rather than missing those conveniences, many people love the simplicity. Cabin people tell fond (and sometimes tall) tales of cold morning encounters with outhouse seats, hauling wood for wood stoves or fireplaces, and meals produced under less-than-ideal circumstances.

Not many of us want to give up our creature comforts permanently, but we can imitate cabin life by consciously simplifying our surroundings. Be on the lookout for pieces that serve more than one purpose. And be selective when choosing accessories. Gizmos have to be maintained and knick-knacks have to be dusted, you know.

Cabins are often furnished with cast-offs collected from a variety of places. To avoid the look of chaos, cabin owners sometimes rely on neutral tones. With a couple of coats of paint or a few yards of fabric, almost any hand-me-down piece can fit in beautifully.

Combining neutral tones with natural textures produces a restful atmosphere. Most of the color in the living room at left is provided by the deep tones and textures of the hardwood floors, massive beams, and brick fireplace. In a room with strong structural elements like this one, all you need to add is lots of warm white paint and fabric in complementary tones for upholstery or slipcovers, pillows, and window treatments.

You can duplicate this effect even without beams and bricks. The keeping room below started with nothing more than spare lines, neutral tones, and stained woodwork. Adding hand-woven baskets and rag rugs, a side chair with a rush seat, and rag balls brought natural shapes and textures into the room. If this look appeals to you, stick to a fairly narrow range of colors and textures, and remember that less is more when simplicity is the goal.

Space is tight in most cabins, so coat racks, hooks, shelves, baskets, and recessed spaces often are used for permanent storage. In the sitting room at left, firewood is stashed beneath the hearth, and books, games, and stereo speakers are shelved near a comfortable rocker. In the eating area below, dishes, tableware, and linens wait beside the dining table. Displayed in a simple cabinet, they add homey bits of color to the room between meals.

The strategies that make it possible to be comfortable in a small cabin will work in any room.

- Store things within easy reach of areas where they're used, and make them part of the decor.
- Take advantage of every recessed space.
- Put attractive hooks on the backs of all bedroom and bathroom doors.
- Use trunks and chests for storage space as well as furniture.

On a windy fall day at the cabin, the kids were trying to rake leaves. Frustrated, they decided to tie a tarp between two trees to protect their pile. The wind caught the tarp and ballooned it out into an enormous parachute that lifted them right off the ground. They screamed, and we ran to help. Pretty soon we were all dangling from ropes and laughing like crazy. I'll never forget that afternoon. Three grown-ups and five kids played together for hours, completely entertained by a cheap plastic tarp and a rope.

Brenda O.

COAT RACK

Home is where you hang your hat…or your jacket!

1 *Find the studs in the wall, and if possible, plan to center the coat rack over a stud. Decide how long the coat rack will be and cut a birch log to fit. (We made ours 48" [1.22 m].) Mark a straight line along the length of each side of the log, and use a circular saw to cut along those marks. If necessary, complete the cut with a hand saw.*

2 *Starting 4" (10.16 cm) from one end, mark and drill evenly spaced ¾" holes for the pegs. Cut the ¾" dowel into pegs, one for each hole. Sand the pegs, rounding over the edges of the ends, and glue one into each hole. Finish the pegs and the faces of the pine buttons to match or complement the coat rack. Apply two coats of polyurethane to the entire piece, front and back, if desired.*

3 *Drill a ⅜" (9.5 mm) hole 2" in from each end of the rack and one in the center. Drill corresponding pilot holes in the wall. Insert a hollow wall anchor into any pilot hole that does not hit a stud. Hold the coat rack against the wall. At each ⅜" hole, drive a 3" wallboard screw through the log and into the wall. Tap the pine buttons into the holes to cover the screwheads.*

MATERIALS:

BIRCH LOG • ¾" (19.1 CM) PINE DOWEL
PINE BUTTONS • WOOD GLUE • PAINT OR STAIN (OPTIONAL)
SATIN-FINISH POLYURETHANE • 3" (7.62 CM) WALLBOARD SCREWS

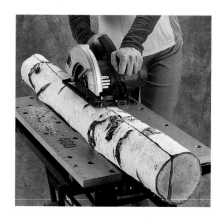  

VINYL FLOOR CLOTH

Bring a Native American theme into a room with
an inexpensive, durable floor cloth.

1 *Cut a 36 × 60" (91.44 cm × 1.52 m) piece of vinyl.
Roll a coat of latex-based primer onto the back of the vinyl.
When the primer is dry, paint the entire floor cloth with
two coats of the base paint.*

2 *Mark the horizontal and vertical centers of the floor
cloth, and transfer the pattern (shown on page 134) onto
it. Mask off the edges of the center medallion; seal the
inside edges of the tape with matte medium and let it dry.
(This keeps the paint from seeping under the tape when
you paint.)*

3 *Paint the center sections of the medallion, let the
paint dry, and remove the tape. Continue masking and
painting one color at a time until the pattern is complete.
Let the paint dry for a week, then add two coats of water-
based polyurethane.*

MATERIALS:
• SCRAP OF SHEET VINYL • LATEX-BASED PRIMER
• MASKING TAPE • MATTE MEDIUM
• ACRYLIC PAINT • WATER-BASED POLYURETHANE

BEAR PAW PLAQUES

Make these fieldstone pawprints with a group of children.
You'll all have fun.

1 *Coat the inside of the form with petroleum jelly. Forms can be
anything from special plastic molds to shallow cardboard boxes to
pine 1 × 2s (2.54 × 5.08 cm) nailed to plywood. Mix water and quick-
setting concrete mix, according to manufacturer's directions. Fill the
molds, use a scrap of lumber to skim off any excess, then smooth the
surface with a trowel.*

2 *Let the concrete dry for 10 minutes, then press an oval stone
into the center and surround it with five pebbles set on edge. Make
sure each stone is partially submerged and firmly settled into the concrete. Let the concrete cure several hours or overnight, then remove it
from the forms.*

NOTE: *These plaques are quite heavy. If you plan to hang them, use
masonry screws to attach heavy-duty hanging hardware.*

MATERIALS:

- CONTAINERS TO BE USED AS FORMS • PETROLEUM JELLY
- RIVER STONES (1 LARGE OVAL AND 5 PEBBLES FOR EACH)
- QUICK-SETTING CONCRETE MIX • DUST MASK

Comfortable cozy, warm

—inside and out…all things good.

What makes you comfortable?

For me, it's warmth, plenty of natural light, soft places to stretch out, lots of color, plus books and reminders of the people I love. Your list would surely be different—everyone's unique.

Talk with your family and compile a list of your own. You might be surprised at what you discover. It's easy to make a room more comfortable, but it's a little like using a road map. First you have to know where you're headed, and a list like this is a good way to define your destination.

With my list in hand, I know my sitting room needs lots of windows with minimal window treatments, a fireplace or wood stove, a big sofa or overstuffed chairs with pillows and ottomans, and at least two walls of floor-to-ceiling shelves. The result is a room that's completely comfortable to me.

Where will your list lead you?

I have great memories of homemade donuts from the donut maker in the mornings, crack of dawn fishing trips with my best friend's dad, sunning out on the dock and having big wet dogs come and shake all over us, and a wonderful wood-burning sauna for cool evenings. Above the fire in the sauna was a basin of rocks that heated up, and we'd pour buckets of water on the rocks to create a steam sauna for an extra treat. This was bath time, and we'd soap up with little pails of water in the warm sauna, then run out and jump off the dock into the cool lake to rinse. We'd go back and forth several times before calling it a night.

Kristen M.

Some comforts are meant for the heart and soul as much as for the body. Antiques, heirlooms, and handmade accessories make a room, such as the reading nook at right, cozy and inviting.

Certain textures add comfort, too. In the bedroom above, the log walls and headboard create a homey atmosphere that is reinforced by the flannels, fleeces, felts, and velvets of the bedding and accessories. Though they're very different in appearance, each of these rooms offers creature comforts tailored to its purpose and to the people who use it.

One other note on comfort: Area rugs are especially valuable on floors made of materials such as hardwood, brick, and stone, which work well in a rustic atmosphere but can be awfully cold on early spring or late fall mornings. No one wants to step out of a warm bed onto a cold, hard floor. Use soft rugs, such as chenille or braided rag rugs beside beds, and lighter, fast-drying rugs in bathrooms and near doorways. Save hard-to-clean wool rugs for areas that are well away from heavy traffic areas.

Cabins are magnets for friends and family, and when you're entertaining a crowd, you need plenty of seating. It's not important that the chairs match. (Take a look at the many different chair styles represented in the great room at left.) It is important that they're comfortable and that some of them are light enough to be moved from one place to another, depending on the number of guests and the activities at hand.

Look for opportunities to add seating to your cabin-style rooms. Even small spaces such as the kitchen above can include a pair of small chairs and cheerful pillows. And remember that sofas and chairs aren't the only options: Trunks, ottomans, and floor cushions come in handy for parties and other large gatherings.

FISH HEADBOARD

A whole new—and pleasant—way to "sleep with the fishes."

1▸ Clamp two cedar 4 × 4 fence posts together and mark cutting lines for the dadoes as shown in the diagram on page 50. Set the cutting depth on a circular saw to exactly match the thickness of the 2 × 4 stringers. Between the lines marked for the dadoes, make cuts across the posts, one cut every ¼" (6.4 mm). Use a chisel to remove the waste material within the dadoes. Set the stringers into position, their ends flush with the outside edges of the posts and their faces flush with the faces of the posts. Secure the stringers with 2½" drywall screws. Thoroughly sand the entire assembly.

2▸ Cut the MDF base and backing, and route the top edges of each with a roundover bit. Apply a coat of primer to both sides and all the edges of each piece, and let it dry. Screw the base to the stringers and countersink the screws. Turn the assembly over and set the backing in place above the first stringer; align it so the top extends ½" (12.7 mm) beyond the top of the base. Drive screws through the backing and into the base.

continued

 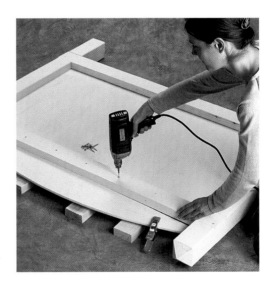

MATERIALS:

- 48" (1.22 M) 4 × 4 (10.16 × 10.16 CM) CEDAR FENCE POSTS (2)
- ¾" (19.1 MM) MDF (ONE 4 × 8 FT. [1.22 × 2.44 M] SHEET) • 2 × 4S (5.08 × 10.16 CM) (2) • 2½" (6.35 CM) DRYWALL SCREWS • TACK CLOTH • LATEX PRIMER • STENCIL MEDIA • STENCIL ADHESIVE • MODELING COMPOUND
- LATEX PAINT • SATIN-FINISH POLYURETHANE • HOLLYWOOD BED FRAME
- 2" (5.08 CM) HEX-HEAD BOLTS

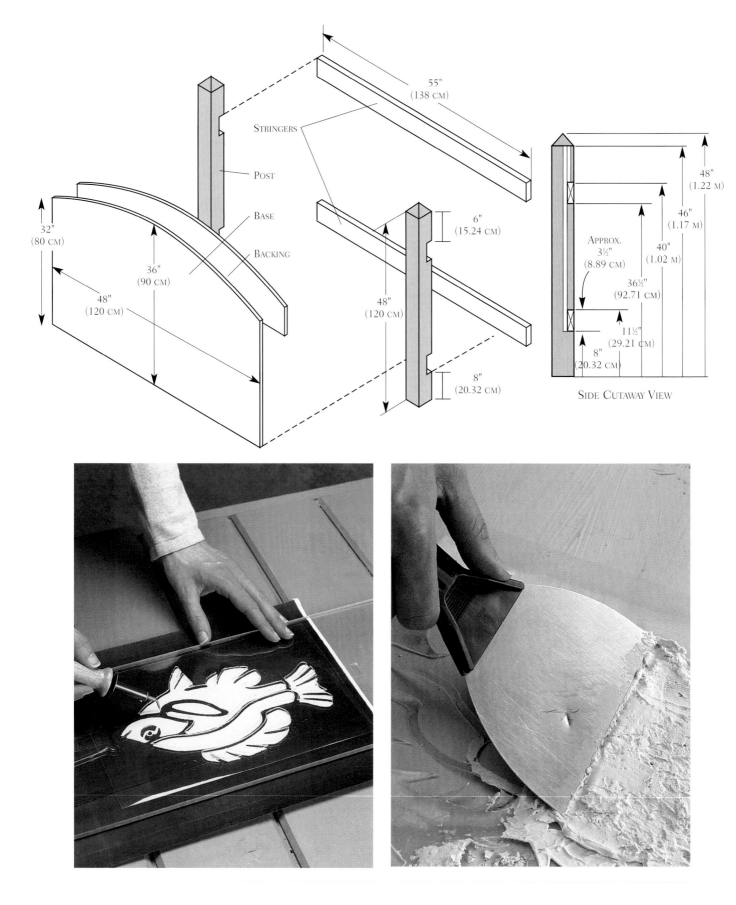

STRINGERS

POST

BASE

BACKING

55"
(138 CM)

32"
(80 CM)

36"
(90 CM)

48"
(120 CM)

6"
(15.24 CM)

48"
(120 CM)

8"
(20.32 CM)

48"
(1.22 M)

46"
(1.17 M)

40"
(1.02 M)

APPROX.
3½"
(8.89 CM)

36½"
(92.71 CM)

11½"
(29.21 CM)

8"
(20.32 CM)

SIDE CUTAWAY VIEW

3 Photocopy and enlarge the pattern on page 135. Set a piece of glass over the pattern, then lay a piece of stencil media over the glass. Cut the stencil, using a stencil burner.

4 Mark the center of the headboard and make placement marks for the design. Spray the back of the stencil with stencil adhesive and secure it to the headboard. Spread a layer of modeling compound across the stencil, taking care to fill in all open areas. While the modeling compound is wet, remove the tape and peel off the stencil. Let the compound dry completely. Add layers until the design is approximately ³⁄₁₆" (4.8 mm) thick. Carefully clean the stencil between applications and make sure each layer is thoroughly dry before adding another. On the last coat, use the putty knife to texture the surface in much the same way you swirl frosting on a cake.

5 Paint the entire headboard with a base coat of soft yellow, and let it dry. Add a coat of soft green glaze. While the glaze is still slightly wet, wipe it with a damp sponge, removing glaze so that the base coat shows through in some areas. Pat the raised design with the sponge, leaving enough paint so that the design is shadowed and emphasized. Let the paint dry completely. (For additional information, see page 129.) Lightly sand selected areas to imitate wear patterns, then wipe away the sanding dust with a tack cloth. Dip an old toothbrush in dark green or black paint and pat it nearly dry on paper towels. Working in one small area at a time, scrape your fingernail across the toothbrush bristles to spatter paint across the headboard. Let the paint spatters dry completely, then seal the entire headboard with two coats of polyurethane.

6 Mark and drill holes in the posts, and then use bolts to attach a Hollywood bed frame to the headboard.

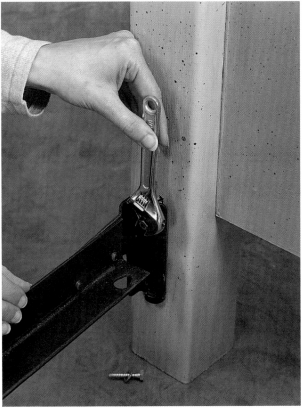

FRINGED SUEDE PILLOW

Add a bit of western flair with a cowboy-inspired ultrasuede pillow.

1 *Cut two 23" (58.42 cm) squares from the brown synthetic suede and a 14" square from the tan. Reproduce the pattern on page 135. Lay out the pattern on one of the dark brown squares and cut it to shape. Use a glue stick to secure the cut-out to the tan square as indicated. Sew fabrics together, stitching close to the edges. Place brass studs (through only the brown layer) as indicated on the template.*

2 *On the right side of the pillow top, place masking tape 3½" (8.89 cm) from each outside edge to mark the length of the fringe. Mark the tape every ¼" (6.4 mm). Match the edges of the squares, wrong sides together, and use paper clips to hold them together. At the outer edge of the tape,*

sew the pillow together, leaving a 14" (35.56 cm) opening in the center of one side. Cut the fringe on the three finished sides. With a straightedge and the marked tape as a guide, cut to within ½" (12.7 mm) of the tape with a rotary cutter, and then use scissors to complete each cut up to, but not through, the stitching. At each corner, cut away the excess fabric (3½" [8.89 cm] squares).

3 *Insert the pillow form, then stitch the remaining side. Cut the fringe as described above. Holding the first fringe strips from both layers together, tie them in an overhand knot. Use a small pair of scissors to slide the knot into position. Tie knots all the way around the pillow; make all of the knots in the same direction.*

MATERIALS:
- ⅔ (60.96 cm) YARD OF BROWN SYNTHETIC SUEDE
- 14" (35.56 cm) PIECE OF TAN SYNTHETIC SUEDE
- 16" (40.64 cm) PILLOW FORM • GLUE STICK
- NARROW MASKING TAPE • 5 mm BRASS STUDS

FLEECE BLANKET

On cool evenings, curl up with this surprisingly easy-to-make polar fleece throw.

1 ▸ *Cut a 72 × 60" (1.83 × 1.52 m) piece of red fleece. Cut off the selvage edges, and round off the corners. Following the diagram on page 134, draw chalk lines across blanket. Cut six ½"-wide (12.7 cm) strips of black fleece. Stretch each strip: Grasp the end firmly with one hand and pull the fabric between the thumb and forefinger of your other hand. As it's stretched, the fleece will curl and develop a chenille-like appearance. Using an open-toe applique foot, and a medium zigzag stitch, sew a stretched strip to each marked line on the blanket. Bar tack at each end to secure the strips.*

2 ▸ *Enlarge the patterns on page 135. Cut out the bear and bear-paw shapes from black fleece. Center the bear within the center diamond and use spray adhesive to hold it in place. Add the bear-paw designs to the corners of adjacent diamonds as shown. Using a straight stitch near the outside edges, sew the bear and bear paws in place.*

3 ▸ *At the outside edges of the blanket, fold ⅜" (9.5 mm) to the wrong side and pin it in place. Blanket stitch the hem, using pearl cotton and a darning needle.*

MATERIALS:

- 2⅛ YARDS (1.94 M) RED SYNTHETIC FLEECE, 60" (1.52 M) WIDE
- ½ YARD (45.72 CM) BLACK SYNTHETIC FLEECE • DRESSMAKER'S CHALK • TEMPORARY FABRIC ADHESIVE • #3 PEARL COTTON, BLACK
- DARNING NEEDLE

Being together, having fun, it just feels
Natural.

As a child, whenever my world disappointed me, I hid in my treehouse, wrapped in the embrace of an enormous oak tree. As a teenager, I retreated to a rock in the middle of a creek at the foot of our property or to a fire tower on top of Dogwood Mountain. These days I seek comfort along dusty trails in the deserts of New Mexico. Nature has always called to me, has always spoken straight to my spirit.

In that way, I'm not unusual. Millions of people find that trees and rocks and water soothe their souls. The popularity of cabins is, in part, testament to nature's power to entertain, energize, and restore the human spirit.

Above all else, it is a connection to nature—through location, building materials, or atmosphere—that transforms a small, rural house into a cabin. And it is a connection to nature that can transform any room into a cabin-style retreat.

As I've said before, the first step is to look within yourself to find the natural materials that are closest to your own heart. Often, you'll find that those materials are the ones found outside your own back door, or the ones found outside the doors of your childhood.

I imagine that the kitchen at left and the foyer below belong to people who live—or once lived (in their imaginations, if not literally)—at the edge of majestic pine forests. The hand-hewn banister speaks of someone who has a reverence for trees, maybe someone who once harvested timber or replanted a forest.

The craftsmanship of this banister may not be available to everyone, but the floors and trim of the entryway and the natural cabinetry of the kitchen certainly are. And in both rooms, the warm glow of the wood sits against light surfaces—an inviting combination.

When I was growing up, my dad ran a lumber business and managed tracts of timber. The forests of the Ozark Mountains that surrounded us were laden with southern yellow pine, oak, walnut, and ash trees. But the trees that my father loved most were clump birch, a species that was decidedly not native to the area.

Every other spring or so, Dad would dig yet another dead clump of birch out of our yard, and plant a new one, determined that this one would make it. He'd carry water and baby those trees something awful, but they never could survive more than one or two merciless Missouri summers. The first time he visited me in Minnesota, where birch are almost as common as mosquitos, Dad was mesmerized by the sight of miles of them, growing wild.

As you might guess, my cabin was filled with furnishings and accessories made of birch. Bark and twigs are easy to work with and fairly easy to come by, even if you don't live where they grow like weeds. (A quick search of the internet should yield you plenty of sources.) Take a look at pages 130 through 133 for information on harvesting and working with twigs and bark.

Disguised with birch bark and twigs, an inexpensive dresser can become a work of art, such as the one above. And although it might be an ambitious project for a beginner, a birch-log bed, such as the one at left, sets a mellow tone for a bedroom.

There are all kinds of ways to work natural elements into your rooms, and not all of them involve cutting down trees or searching for shed antlers.

The bamboo mirror and shelf unit in the bathroom at right adds a nice, natural touch. And the wildlife theme of the ceramic tile feels just right for a cabin or cabin-style room. In the great room above, wicker furniture and baskets meld with the stone fireplace and hearth, as well as with the neutral tones of the barn siding, to produce an atmosphere that's natural but refined.

Expand your definition of natural materials to include a full range of possibilities, and shop for furniture and accessories with those possibilities in mind.

BIRCH TREE TABLE

Transform birch plywood and branches into a fanciful table for your bedside or entryway. (See page 130 for information on harvesting trees for this project.)

1 Rough cut two 30" sections of a tree trunk, using a bow saw. Cut the branches to similar lengths, then turn the trunk upside down on a flat work surface. Trim branches until the trunk is stable and nearly vertical. Using a scrap 2 × 4 (5.08 × 10.16 cm) as a gauge, scribe the end of each branch for a plumb cut. Trim the branches with a jig saw or reciprocating saw.

2 Set the trunks back on the level surface, mark a height of 25" (63.5 cm) all the way around each one, and use a reciprocating saw to trim them. Set the trunks together. Experiment with arrangements until the branches are interwoven in an interesting pattern and the tops of the trunks are butted or nearly butted together. Find three or four places where the trunks and branches meet, drill pilot holes, and screw the pieces together, using 3 to 4" wallboard screws. If necessary, sand the trunks until the tops are level with one another.

3 Cut a 22"-diameter (55.88 cm) circle from the birch plywood. Cut 1"-diameter branches into about 75 pieces, each 2" (5.08 cm) long. Place the tabletop upside down on a level work surface. Spread wood glue along several inches at a time, and tack twigs in place to cover the edge. Place the twig pieces so the tops are flush with the tabletop and the edges are butted together as closely as possible.

4 Place the tabletop on the trunks, adjust until the tabletop is stable, then trace the positions of the trunks onto the bottom of the tabletop. Remove the tabletop and drill a pilot hole at the center of the marking for each trunk. Spread wood glue on top of each trunk, replace the tabletop, and fasten it to the base with 2" wallboard screws. Fill and sand the holes for the screws. Paint the tabletop a cream color to complement the birch bark, then seal the entire piece with polyurethane varnish, if desired.

MATERIALS:

• WELL-DRIED, SPREADING TREE TRUNK SECTIONS, APPROXIMATELY 30" (76.2 CM) (2) • 3 TO 4" (7.62 TO 10.16 CM) WALLBOARD SCREWS • ¾" (19.1 MM) BIRCH VENEER PLYWOOD • VARIETY OF 1" (2.54 CM) BIRCH BRANCHES • WOOD GLUE • 1" (2.54 CM) BRADS • 2" (5.08 CM) WALLBOARD SCREWS • WOOD PUTTY • WATER-BASED, SATIN-FINISH POLYURETHANE

BIRCH LOG FLOOR LAMP

Light up your life with this perfectly natural floor lamp.

1 For the base, cut a 15" (38.1 cm) circle of plywood, and drill a ⅜" (9.5 mm) hole in the center. Route the edge with an ogee bit, if desired. Paint the base and toy wheels with acrylic paint. Put a flat washer, lock washer, and a hex nut onto one end of the threaded nipple. Insert the nipple up through the center of the base, and tighten the hex nut to set the lock washer.

2 Cut four 10"-long (25.4 cm) birch logs. Use a ½" (12.7 mm) auger bit to drill a hole through the center of each log. Slide two toy wheels onto the nipple, and add a log. Continue alternating between sets of toy wheels and logs, ending with two toy wheels. Top the wheels with a brass cap, then thread the brass couplers onto the nipple. Approximately ½" (12.7 mm) of the nipple should extend beyond the last coupler.

3 Top the nipple with a threaded brass washer and then a harp; attach a socket cap. Pull the lamp cord through the nipple and into the socket cap. Tie the split ends of the wire in an underwriter's knot, connect them to the lamp socket, and assemble the socket (see page 126). Add a lamp shade and, if you like, a finial.

MATERIALS:

• ¾" (19.1 MM) BIRCH PLYWOOD • 2" (5.08 CM) WOODEN TOY WHEELS (12) • DARK BROWN ACRYLIC PAINT
• ¾" (19.1 MM) DRYWALL SCREWS • 52" (132.08 CM) THREADED NIPPLE • 2 TO 2½"-DIAMETER (5.08 TO 6.35 CM) BIRCH BRANCHES
• FLAT WASHER (1) • LOCK WASHER (1) • HEX NUT (1) • BRASS CAP (1) • 1" (2.54 CM) BRASS COUPLERS (3) • THREADED BRASS
WASHER (1) • HARP • SOCKET CAP • LAMP SOCKET • LAMP CORD • LAMP SHADE

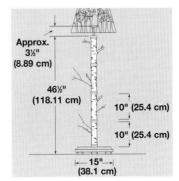

Approx. 3½" (8.89 cm)

46½" (118.11 cm)

10" (25.4 cm)

10" (25.4 cm)

15" (38.1 cm)

LAMP SHADES

Add atmosphere with embellished lamp shades.

SHADOWED SHADE:

Cut simple shapes, such as pine trees or pine cones, bears, or moose from plain white paper. Apply spray adhesive to one side of the shapes and press them inside the lampshade.

FEATHERED SHADE:

Hot glue peacock feathers around a simple shade. If you like, add a row of ribbon to the top and the bottom edges of the shade.

BEJEWELED SHADE:

Punch evenly spaced holes around the lower edge of a paper shade. Cut 7" (17.78 cm) lengths of 16-gauge copper wire. For each wire: form a coil at one end—five tight revolutions around a piece of ⁵⁄₃₂" (4 mm) brass tubing. Slide a bead onto the other end, then form a single loop. (We wrapped the wire once around a ½"-diameter [12.7 mm] marker.) Slide the loop through a hole in the lampshade, then crimp the end of the loop to close it. Hot glue small stones, pinecones, feathers, and so forth to the wire coils.

MATERIALS:

• ASSORTED LAMP SHADES • HOT GLUE • PEACOCK FEATHERS
• 16-GAUGE (1.5 MM) COPPER WIRE • SIMPLE BEADS • SMALL STONES,
PINECONES, FEATHERS, AND OTHER NATURAL ITEMS • WHITE PAPER
• SPRAY ADHESIVE

  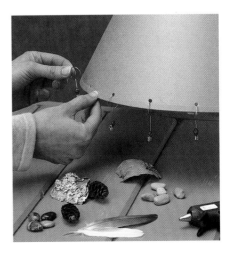

The minute we step through the door, we're
Relaxed.

Years ago I read a story about a man whose lawn was worn down by daily games of baseball and soccer. In response to neighborhood criticism, he said, "I'm raising children here, not grass."

I reminded myself of those words a thousand times during my children's growing up years, and I mention them here because that attitude is the epitome of cabin style. In homes where it's clear that people are more important than things, it's easy to relax.

Cabin living is fairly informal. (How formal can you be wearing a swimsuit and shorts from sunrise to sunset?) Cabins have no room for don't-touch-me furniture or extremely delicate accessories. Instead, most are furnished with durable fabrics, rugged materials, and weathered fin-

ishes that leave their inhabitants free from concerns about the wear and tear of everyday living. Those same elements can set the stage for carefree living in your home.

Most cabins are eclectic—another word for "nothing matches"—because they're often furnished with combinations of family hand-me-downs and cast-offs collected from many sources. Cabin-style rooms are, by nature, eclectic as well, but they work best when the pieces are loosely related through color or style or shape. This strategy produces rooms that are informal, but not chaotic.

Symmetry, shape, and color link the various pieces in the bathroom at left. For example, the mirror frames don't match, but they're connected by their rectangular shapes and similar finish colors. And take a look at how they're hung. Their tops are level with the tops of the sconces and

with one another, and they're equidistant from the window. With so many things in common, you have to look twice before you realize how different they are.

The porch below really invites you to sit down and relax, doesn't it? With this view, it would be hard to go wrong, but there are things we can learn from this room, even if we don't have that lake or those trees right outside our windows. The colors and textures in the pine logs of the porch walls and floor are echoed in each piece of furniture, and the diamond patterns from the rug are repeated in the lamp. The key here is repetition of materials, shapes, and colors…not to mention those windows.

Slipcovers work magic in informal rooms. They can be used to camouflage a piece that's worn or just plain ugly, or to soften upholstered pieces that are too formal. They can even change with the seasons. Many slipcovers can be dry cleaned or carefully laundered—a big plus in rooms where lots of activities take place and food may be served.

In the charming room at left, contrasting piping on the slipcovers pulls the mismatched prints and pillows together. This mixture creates the impression of pieces inherited or gathered over time, an essential aspect of cabin style.

The sofa above is another example of the softening effect of slipcovers. It's covered in an assortment of vintage fabrics, loosely related to one another through color and style.

In a relaxed atmosphere, things can be adapted or converted to meet the most pressing need. In the dining area at left, the chandelier was hung near the ceiling to preserve the magnificent view. Recessed lights in the area supplement the lighting scheme at night or on dreary days.

The oversized twig chairs work fine with the table, and they can be used in the nearby great room when the need arises. All of the chairs in the room have cushions or pillows, which makes them even more inviting.

Making do with what's on hand can result in charming rooms, such as the bedroom below. Here, old shutters form a headboard and area rugs imitate carpeting. A small footstool holds odds and ends at the foot of the bed, and an overly-bright floor lamp is softened with a handful of vintage linens draped over the shade. Looks like a great place to curl up with a good book and a cup of hot cocoa on a chilly morning, doesn't it?

The carpet in our cabin was selected to match the dirt in the yard so no one would feel bad if they tracked up the floor with muddy hunting boots. My brother, Paul, smeared a bunch of dirt samples from the road and yard onto a board and took the board with him when he went carpet shopping. He picked the carpet that was closest to the color of the dirt. And you know, after 20 years of hunting trips with at least a dozen guys, that carpet still looks okay.

Ben O.

LOG SLICE OTTOMAN

Rest your feet or a snack tray on this simple ottoman.

1 Cut a 16 to 20" (40.64 to 50.8 cm) slice of a tree trunk. Hand plane the top until it's smooth and even. Set the log upside down on a level work surface, and use a carpenter's square to mark a consistent cutting line. Start this cut with a circular saw, following the line around the log; finish with a reciprocating saw or hand saw. Sand the top with a fine-grade sanding sponge. Remove any sawdust, dirt, or debris from the bark with a stiff-bristled brush, then apply two coats of varnish to the bark and cut surfaces. Let the varnish dry.

2 Drill pilot holes and attach three equally spaced casters to the bottom of the log.

MATERIALS:

• LARGE TREE TRUNK OR LOG • FINE-GRADE SANDING SPONGE
• WATER-BASED, SATIN-FINISH POLYURETHANE VARNISH
• CASTERS (3)

INDIAN BLANKET PILLOW

Pair denim with rugged Indian blanket fabric for a floor pillow that will stand up to years of everyday use.

1 *Cut one rectangle of denim fabric, 37 × 26" (93.98 × 66.04 cm). Cut a piece of blanket fabric, 30½ × 26" (77.47 × 66.04 cm). Finish the raw edge of the blanket fabric, using a zigzag stitch. To create an inner flap, fold 6" (15.24 cm) of the blanket fabric to the wrong side and press the fold.*

2 *Fold the denim rectangle in half lengthwise with the right sides together and the raw edges matching. Stitch a ½" (12.7 mm) seam from the raw edges to the fold. Press the seam open to a point. Turn the stitched end right side out, centering the seam to make a flap as shown. Press the folded edges of the flap, then finish the lower edge of the flap facing, using a zigzag stitch.*

3 *Stitch the facing of the denim flap in place 1" (2.54 cm) from the lower edge, through both layers. Fold the flap down along the stitching line, and press it. Layer the fabrics, right sides together, and stitch the denim fabric to the blanket fabric with a ½" seam allowance; press the seam open. Align the folds, and bring the flap of blanket fabric to the opposite side, enclosing the denim flap. Match the raw edges and pin the sides together. Stitch 1" seams on both sides, then trim the seam allowances to ½".*

4 *Turn the pillow cover right side out. Center the concho on the denim flap, then mark and make two small buttonholes. Insert the pillow form, and tuck it into the inner flap. Cut a 24" (60.96 cm) piece of suede lacing, thread each end through a buttonhole, and tie the ends together. Thread the lacing through the slits in the suede ornament, and then through the concho. Tie the lacing together to keep the concho in place, then knot the ends.*

Note: The blanket fabric we used is Ralph Lauren's Retreat Navaho in Lake Blue.

MATERIALS:

- 1 YD (.95 M) OF 48 TO 60" (1.22 TO 1.52 M) FABRIC
- 1 YD (.95 M) OF BLANKET FABRIC
- 24" (60.96 CM) SQUARE PILLOW FORM
- SUEDE ORNAMENT • SUEDE LACING • SILVER CONCHO

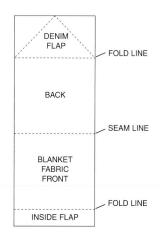

DENIM FLAP — FOLD LINE

BACK

— SEAM LINE

BLANKET FABRIC FRONT

— FOLD LINE

INSIDE FLAP

DOOR BENCH

The small, design-friendly frames of five-panel doors are just right for this simple bench.

As you shop for doors, keep these tips in mind:

• doors should be roughly the same overall width, height, and thickness
• panel openings should be the same size
• stile and rail widths should be the same and milling details should be similar

Following our plans, each five-panel door yields three full-sized frame-and-panel units where the frame is full width on all four sides. Before you begin cutting, consider the placement of hinge or lockset mortises and other features of the doors.

Material	Part	No.	Dimensions
Three-panel frame	Back	1	28 × 49" (71.12 cm × 1.24 m)
Single-panel frames	Ends	2	17½ × 30" (44.45 × 76.2 cm)
Single-panel frames	Seat	2	17½ × 24½" (44.45 × 62.23 cm)
Single-panel frames	Kickboards	2	17½ × 24½" (44.45 × 62.23 cm)
2 × 4s	Frame supports	4	46" (1.17 m)
2 × 4s	Frame supports	4	14" (35.56 cm)
1 × 3s	Armrests	2	18½" (46.99 cm)

If it's not possible to match these dimensions from the doors you select, follow these guidelines: For the back, select a door that has a three-panel section that equals the width of two seat-panel frames, end-to-end. (If necessary, trim the stiles of the seat panels to match.) The middle stile sections, where the seat and kick panels meet, should combine to equal one full stile width. The width of the end panels should accommodate the depth of the seat panels plus the thickness of the back panel. (This can be adjusted by including some overhang on the front edge of the seat panels.)

MATERIALS:
FIVE-PANEL DOORS (3) • 8 FT. (2.44 M) 2 × 4S (5.08 × 10.16 CM) (2)
• 40" (1.02 M) 1 × 3 (2.54 × 7.62 CM)
• #10 2½" (6.35 CM) WOOD SCREWS • WOOD GLUE
• PRIMER • LATEX ENAMEL PAINT, BLACK

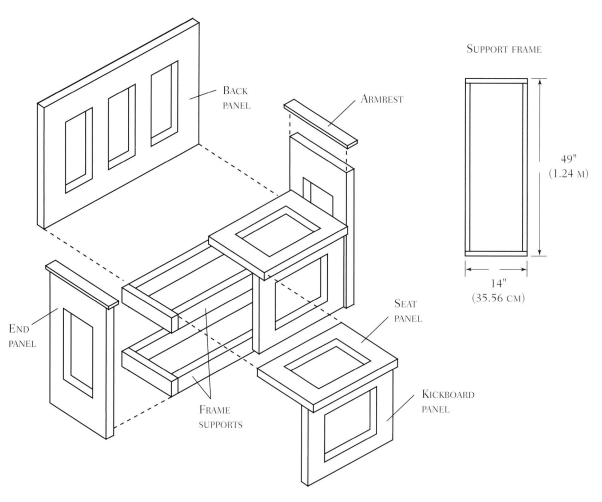

BACK PANEL

ARMREST

SUPPORT FRAME

49"
(1.24 M)

14"
(35.56 CM)

END PANEL

SEAT PANEL

FRAME SUPPORTS

KICKBOARD PANEL

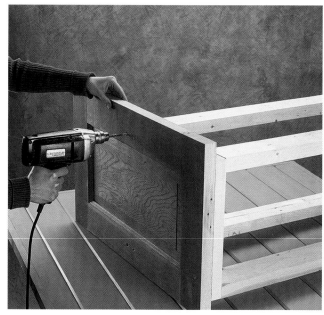

1 Remove any hardware remaining on the doors, then mark them, and use a straightedge and circular saw to cut parts as indicated on page 83. Compare the overall lengths of the back panel, seat and kick panel combinations. Adjust as necessary, then sand all edges. (If any of the frame joints come apart when you cut the doors, simply reglue the joints, clamp them together, and set them aside to dry.)

2 Following the diagram at left, lay out and assemble the 2 × 4 support frames. Use 2½" wood screws to secure the joints. Mark the seat and support frame positions on the end panels. Drill counterbored pilot holes and fasten end panels to the support frames, using glue and 2½" wood screws.

3 Position the back, drill pilot holes, and secure it, again using glue and wood screws. Next, install both seat pieces and both kickboards.

4 Position the 1 × 3 armrests over the end panels, with the edges flush along the insides of the panels, and the ends flush at the back of the bench, leaving a 1" (2.54 cm) overhang at the front. Attach the armrests with glue and wood screws.

5 Fill and sand the screw holes. Paint the bench with primer and two coats of black paint, allowing the paint to dry thoroughly between coats.

At the cabin, it's always time for Fun.

At eight years old, my daughter, Katie, loved going to the cabin. "The cabin is my best place," she once said. "No one's ever in a hurry there, and it's always time for fun."

When we leave ordinary life behind, we give ourselves permission to have fun. Play is essential to our well-being, yet most of us find time for what we think we have to do by giving up the things we merely want to do. But at a cabin, away from alarm clocks and phones and computers, without errands to run and car pool schedules to keep, we play outside with our family and our friends. We find time to read, play board games, and work with our hands.

Redecorating alone won't create a cabin atmosphere in our homes. Most of us also need to slow down and make time for good, old-fashioned fun.

Most of us also need to set aside a little room for fun. Start by keeping games, books, and hobby materials in plain sight, near where the action is. (Out of sight, out of mind, you know.) With the addition of a console table, some shelves, and a couple of chairs, the hallway above becomes an artist's workspace. Casually but neatly organized, these art supplies don't take up much room and yet they're ready whenever the artist has a minute.

The porch on the right is a natural place for storing paraphernalia for all sorts of fun, such as fishing, gardening, and games. Here, the gear not only looks great, it creates a constant invitation to make time for fun. What a great idea.

Fun is where you find it. Some people—and I am definitely one of them—think reading is fun. Others prefer athletic activities. Still others love the thrill of the hunt for wildlife or for collector's items and flea market treasures. Whatever your passions, surround yourself with their accoutrements. That way, your equipment will be ready at a moment's notice, and more importantly, you'll be living in the midst of the things you love.

The things a person chooses to display offer clues to his or her interests and personality. The bedroom walls above are adorned with books, and a group of pillows made of vintage fabrics nestle on the bed. This room looks as if it belongs to a woman who reads and gardens and sews, just a little.

The fireplace at left is home to vintage sports gear of all sorts. The family who lives here could include a couple who fish in the summer, hunt in the fall, and play in the snow in the winter. They probably like to spend Saturday mornings at flea markets and never miss a good estate sale.

What do your rooms say about you and what you do for fun? If you're not sure, maybe it's time to bring more of yourself into your rooms.

CHECKERBOARD

Keep this framed checkerboard hanging around—it's always ready for a quick game.

1 ▷ Cut a 20 × 20" (50.8 × 50.8 cm) square of MDF for the base. For the frame, rip 2½"-wide (6.35 cm) strips of plywood; cut the plywood strips and the crown molding into four 24" (60.96 cm) sections each. Using the base as a guide, cut the plywood strips to fit, mitering the ends at 45°. Clamp the strips in place and label them for placement.

2 ▷ Using the board and frame as a guide, cut the inner crown molding to fit, mitering the ends at 45°. Label these pieces for placement as well.

3 ▷ Seal all the pieces with pigmented shellac, and let them dry. Set the base on a level surface, on top of ¼" (6.4 mm) spacers. Reassemble the plywood pieces as marked, drill pilot holes, and nail the plywood to the base. Spread glue on the backs of the crown molding pieces, reassemble them as marked, and clamp them in place. Drill pilot holes, and nail the crown molding to the base.

4 ▷ Apply a coat of red paint to the entire assembly, and let it dry. Apply antiquing glaze to the frame and molding, and let it stand for about five minutes. Use the stippling brush to remove some of the glaze from the frame, then let it dry for at least an hour. Apply antiquing glaze to the board and immediately wipe it away with a cotton rag. Let the board dry overnight.

5 ▷ Following the directions on page 128, create a stencil for the checkerboard. Using the stencil, antiquing glaze, and a stencil brush, lightly paint the first set of squares. When the glaze is dry, turn the stencil 180° and paint the remaining squares. Let the board dry overnight. Cut 24" (60.96 cm) lengths of ruling tape, and apply them to the board as indicated on the pattern.

MATERIALS:

- ¾" (19.1 MM) MDF • ⅜" (9.5 MM) SOLID-CORE PLYWOOD
- CROWN MOLDING (8 FT. [2.44 M])
- PIGMENTED SHELLAC • ¼" PLYWOOD SCRAPS FOR SPACERS
- 6D FINISH NAILS • WOOD GLUE • LATEX PAINT (RED)
- BLACK ANTIQUING GLAZE • STIPPLING BRUSH
- TAGBOARD • ⅛" (3.2MM) BLACK RULING TAPE

BOOKSHELVES

Store books and games—big parts of the cabin lifestyle—on these clever shelves.

1 Cut a piece of 2 × 4 6" (15.24 cm) shorter than the width of the door you've selected. Mark a line on the board, 1⅜" (3.49 cm) from the long edge. Set the bevel on a circular saw to 45° and cut along the marked line. Cut the pieces into two sets of cleats. Use 2½" drywall screws to attach the cleats to the back of the door, with the angled point facing down, one at the top and one at the bottom. Hold the door in place and mark the wall at the location of the mating cleats. Screw the cleats to the wall, with the angled point facing up. Be sure you hit a stud or use hollow wall anchors designed to support the combined weight of the door and bookshelves.

2 Determine the placement, size, and number of shelves that are appropriate for your door. (We used two.) Cut 1 × 12 lumber to size and rout the edges of each shelf, using an ogee bit. Finish the shelves to match or complement the door and let them dry.

Mark placement lines for the shelves and for the brackets, marking brackets below each shelf, 2" (5.08 cm) from each end. Drill pilot holes, and attach the brackets beneath the placement lines for the shelves, using ¾" drywall screws. Put the shelves in place, drill pilot holes, and attach brackets to the shelves. Attach the book shelf to the wall.

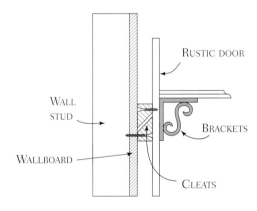

RUSTIC DOOR

WALL STUD

BRACKETS

WALLBOARD

CLEATS

MATERIALS:

• RUSTIC DOOR • 2 × 4 (5.08 × 10.16 CM) • 2½" (6.35 CM) DRYWALL SCREWS • WROUGHT-IRON BRACKETS (2 PER SHELF)
• 1 × 12 (2.54 × 30.48 CM) FINISH-GRADE LUMBER • PAINT OR STAIN AND WATER-BASED, SATIN-FINISH POLYURETHANE
• ¾" (19.1 MM) DRYWALL SCREWS

BIRCH BARK VASE

With a tin can to hold the water, birch bark
becomes a perfectly natural vase.

*1 Peel the bark from the birch log or select an appropriate piece. (See
page 131 for information on peeling birch bark.) If necessary, soak the
bark in water until it's flexible. Wrap the bark around the tin can and
mark it for cutting. Trim the bark to size, using a utility knife. On both
sides of the seam, ¾" (19.1 mm) from the edge, mark and punch evenly
spaced holes, approximately ¾" apart. Hot glue a 1¼" (3.18 cm) strip of
bark, wrong side out, to the top of the rectangle, then punch evenly
spaced holes ¾" (19.1 mm) from the top edge, through both layers of bark.*

*2 Run a bead of hot glue around the back of the bark, wrap it around
the tin can, and use rubber bands to hold it in place. Form the vine into a
circle and clip it to the top edge. Tie a piece of lacing to the vine, and
thread the lacing through the first hole. Wrap the lacing over the vine and
up through the holes in the bark, all the way around the can. At the joint,
wrap the lacing to the inside and knot it. At the seam, thread the lacing
through the pre-punched holes, alternating from one side to the other. At
the end of the seam, bring the lacing to the wrong side of the bark and
knot it.*

MATERIALS:

• TIN CAN, 64-OUNCE (1.9-L) SIZE • BIRCH LOG OR PIECES OF BARK • LEATHER LACING OR RAFFIA
• HOLE PUNCH • FLEXIBLE VINE OR WILLOW TWIG, AT LEAST 18" (45.72 CM) LONG • HOT GLUE

Generations of our family haved loved this place.

It's simply

Timeless.

When my children were small, they loved Marsha Wilson Chall's wonderful book, *Up North at the Cabin*. In it, Chall paints glowing word pictures of the pleasures that await a young girl when she and her family go "up North." She describes watching the loons, listening to the bellow of a moose, and learning to water ski. And, best of all, the girl shares these adventures with her extended family.

It's a story repeated throughout North America: Grandparents retire to a cabin in the woods or on a lake, which they plan for their children to inherit in time. As the grandchildren grow up, the cabin is a constant in their lives, a place where they hope to retire some day. And so the cycle continues.

In many families, cabins are connections to the past and promises for the future. Heirlooms, memorabilia, photographs, and even hunting and fishing trophies collected through the generations are a large part of their timeless appeal. This is an aspect of cabin style that's easy to adopt: Furnish and accessorize your rooms with reminders of the people you love and the special moments you've shared.

I love quilts and think that every cabin or cabin-style home needs at least a couple. Old or new, quilts are tributes to the indomitable spirit of pioneer women. At a time when no one had time or money for anything frivolous, anything merely beautiful, women developed an artform that resulted in a practical necessity. Each quilter shared what she had—fabric scraps or patterns or knowledge— and the results were more than any one person could have accomplished alone. It was this spirit that made possible the exploration and settlement of western North America, and it is truly timeless.

Whether you make them, buy them, or have inherited them; whether you display them on your beds as in the bedroom at right, on your walls, or in a cabinet, include one or two—more if possible. There are too many patterns to even begin to mention all the good ones, but the log cabin pattern is particularly appropriate in a cabin-style room. There are at least a dozen possible settings (arrangements of blocks), but the one displayed in the bedroom above is known as barn raising. You can see another log cabin setting in the quilt project that starts on page 106.

The bedroom below shows how well antiques work in cabin-style rooms. If your antiques are treasures that have been handed down through generations of your family, that's wonderful. They are precious connections to your personal past. But even if you bought a piece at auction recently, it holds memories of your conquest as well as stories of some unknown family. Those stories are connections to our common history, to a past that unites us all.

Another great thing about antiques is that they've already proven their durability. If a chest has survived a hundred years of use and maybe even an ocean voyage or a cross-country trip in a wagon, it surely will survive the rough-and-tumble antics of your children.

Use your antiques, even the ones that seem fragile, such as the tea set at left. Make your treasures part of your family's story so that both the treasures and the stories will be cherished by generations to come.

My best friend's grandparents own neighboring cabins, and I was lucky enough to spend time up there as a teen. One of the best things inside the main cabin was a hallway covered with pictures chronicling the years. A grandkid's first fish, first time up on water skis, birthday celebrations, reunions with old friends, repair projects, hunting seasons, funny moments. It was a wonderful wall of history with a story to go with every picture. If you look closely, you will see my best friend and me at age 13, doing our famous lopsided "synchronized" water ski-ballet routine.

Kristen M.

BIRCH BARK FRAME

Birch bark frames are perfect for photos of outdoor activities.

1 Measure the width and length of the frame's opening and add 5" (12.7 cm) to each. Cut a hardboard rectangle equal to those dimensions. Mark the picture opening on the rectangle. Drill a ½" (12.7 mm) hole at each corner. (To avoid breakout, use a backer board as you drill.) Cut along the marked lines with a jig saw and a fine-toothed blade. Clean out the corners with a sharp chisel, then straighten the inside edges with a flat file.

2 Sand the picture frame, then glue the hardboard to it. Wipe away excess glue with a damp sponge. Seal the entire assembly with pigmented shellac. When the shellac is dry, add a coat of latex enamel.

3 Cut an oversized piece of birch bark to cover the hardboard. (For information on peeling birch bark, see page 131.) Coat the back of the birch bark and the front of the hardboard with contact cement, let each dry slightly, and press the layers together. When the glue is dry, use a utility knife to trim the edges.

4 Cut several ³⁄₁₆"-wide (4.8 mm) strips of bark—enough to cover the edges of the hardboard. Tape these strips (wrong side up) to a piece of paper, and coat them with contact cement. Coat the edges of the frame with contact cement, then cover them with strips of bark. Start on the outside edge and work in one direction, trimming as you go.

MATERIALS:

- ⅛" (3.2 MM) HARDBOARD • PIGMENTED SHELLAC • LATEX ENAMEL PAINT
- INEXPENSIVE PICTURE FRAME • WOOD GLUE • BIRCH BARK • CONTACT CEMENT

LOG CABIN QUILT

The colors of nature—trees, water, and earth—ripple across this log cabin quilt.

1 Straighten the cut ends of the fabric, and trim away the selvages. Cut 2" (5.08 cm) strips across the width of each fabric. Cut 80 two-inch squares from an assortment of neutral fabrics, 16 two-inch squares of green, and 32 two-inch squares each of blue and red. Organize the strips and squares by color.

2 To assemble the log cabin blocks, follow the progression shown in the diagrams below. Use ¼" (6.4 mm) seams throughout. Sew two 2" squares together; designate one color as the top and the other as the bottom. Press the seam allowance toward the darker square. Add a strip of the bottom color, trimming it so the unit is square. Press the seam allowance toward the newly added strip. Add a strip of the top color. Continue around the block, adding strips as shown.

Piece blocks in the following combinations:

greens on the top and neutrals on the bottom (8);

neutrals on the top and greens on the bottom (8);

neutrals on the top and blues on the bottom (16);

blues on the top and neutrals on the bottom (16);

neutrals on the top and reds on the bottom (16);

reds on the top and neutrals on the bottom (16).

Note: The squares are not interchangeable. There is one more strip of the top color than the bottom color.

For the most part, use large-scale prints for the smaller strips of the blocks, and evenly distribute lighter and darker prints within each color. Remember, though, that rules are made to be broken, and that a few exceptions create points of focus.

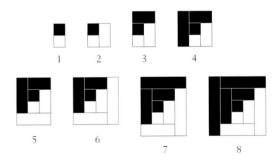

MATERIALS:

• BACKING FABRIC (5¼ YARDS) (5.0 M) • GREEN, BLUE, AND WINE-RED FABRIC, SCRAPS OR ¼ YARD (22.86 CM) CUTS (AT LEAST 10 PIECES OF EACH)

• NEUTRAL, YELLOW, AND PALE GOLD FABRIC, SCRAPS OR ¼ YARD CUTS (AT LEAST 15)

• THIN COTTON BATTING • BINDING FABRIC (¾ YARD [68.58 CM])

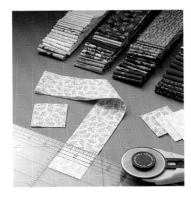

◆ 3 ◆ Lay out the first eight blocks, alternating the greens and neutrals to create the zigzag effect. Add rows, following the diagram on page 107. Arrange the blocks so the colors and patterns are nicely balanced across the rows. When you're satisfied with the layout, sew the eight blocks of each row together, and then sew the 10 rows together, top to bottom. Finger press the seams in opposite directions.

◆ 4 ◆ Press the quilt top and backing fabric. Cut a backing 4" (10.16 cm) wider and longer than the quilt top. (Use special backing fabric or piece narrower fabric to fit.) Layer the quilt top, batting, and backing, and use basting stitches to divide the quilt into quadrants. Working on one quadrant at a time, pin the layers of the quilt together, using safety pins spaced no more than 6" (15.24 cm) apart in parallel rows, vertically and horizontally. Pin the backing over the batting and the edges of the quilt top.

◆ 5 ◆ Attach a walking foot to your machine and adjust the stitch length to 8 to 10 stitches per inch. Stitch-in-the-ditch to quilt the horizontal and vertical rows of blocks: Start near the center and work toward the outside edges. It's best to stitch all the seams in one direction, and then turn the quilt to stitch the seams in the other direction. Next, attach a darning foot, drop the machine's feed dogs, and freehand quilt, following the lines between the light and dark portions of each block.

◆ 6 ◆ Lay the quilt on a flat surface and remove the pins holding the backing over the edges. Pin through all the layers, then machine or hand baste around the quilt, ⅛" (3.2 mm) from the outer edge; remove the pins. Trim the edges,

removing the excess batting and backing. Keep the edges straight and the corners square.

7 Measure all four sides of the quilt. Cut 1¾" (4.45 cm) binding strips from the crosswise width of the fabric. Cut enough strips to equal the quilt's measurement plus a 12" (30.48 cm) working allowance. To join two strips, pin them, right sides together, at right angles. Mark a diagonal line from the corner of the upper strip to the corner of the lower strip. Stitch on the marked line. Trim the seam allowances to ¼" (6.4 mm). Press the seam open. Press the binding strips in half lengthwise, wrong sides together.

8 Choose a starting point along any side of the quilt, and adjust it until none of the seams in the binding fall at corners of the quilt. Leave a 4" (10.16 cm) tail, and line up the raw edges of the strip with the raw edges of the quilt. With a ¼" seam allowance, stitch the binding to the quilt. Stop when you reach the seam allowance of the first corner (¼" from the edge); sew a few backstitches and take the quilt out of the machine. Diagonally fold the binding strip up, and away from the quilt, then fold it straight down, even with the edge of the quilt. Continue stitching to the next corner and finish it in the same manner. When you're within 6 to 8" (15.24 to 20.32 cm) of the starting point, take the quilt out of the machine, adjust the tails to fit and sew them diagonally in the same way you joined the binding. Finish sewing the binding to the quilt. Fold the binding to the wrong side and pin it in place. Slip stitch the binding to the backing until you reach a corner. In the corners, fold the binding to form a miter and continue stitching.

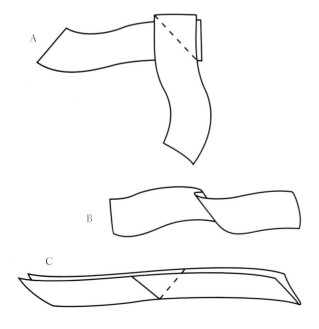

Welcoming us like an old friend —the magic enfolds us.

My most enduring memory of our old cabin is how it reached out to welcome us. Approaching by boat at night, the lighted windows beckoned across the darkened bay. At the driveway, a sign and a 6-ft. hand-carved gnome invited friends and family to enter "Gnome's Hollow." At the water's edge, flags and flowers waved a friendly hello to everyone who passed. The house always felt as if it knew a secret that it was willing to share.

Finally, more than a decade later, I fully understand its magic: There was a place at the cabin for everyone, whether it was one person seeking solitude or a crowd ready for a weekend of sun and fun.

A cabin-style home should welcome you and your family and guests in the same spirit. Put up signs, plant flowers, light lamps and candles, hang wreaths, and display other traditional symbols of hospitality. Create rooms that say, "Come on in. We're so glad you're here." But don't forget to reserve some quiet spaces—comfortable, peaceful areas where you can, as Anne Sexton says, "put your ear down next to your soul and listen hard."

Porches, front doors, and entryways are key players in creating a welcoming atmosphere. A good porch invites you to, as they say down home, "come sit a spell." Chairs such as the ones above, or love seats with soft cushions and a quilt or afghan, such as the one at right, make a good first impression. So do plants and other accessories, such as the sculpture in the corner.

Front doors with glass—particularly sidelights—feel welcoming, maybe because they give visitors a glimpse into the world within even before the door is opened. A sign above or beside a door, or a wreath hanging on it adds a special touch as well.

Entryways present excellent opportunities to make guests comfortable. At a minimum, you'll want to include:

• a mirror, which reflects light and gives visitors a last minute chance to check their appearances.

• tables or other horizontal surfaces to set things people might be carrying.

• a coat rack or hooks.

• a place to sit while removing shoes or boots.

In my suburban neighborhood, as in many others, trick-or-treating is a highly anticipated event. The porch light is a universal signal of welcome for the little ghosts and goblins, one that even the youngest child understands. "Don't go to that house," I once heard a very small child say. "Their lights are off."

Light is so important to a warm welcome. For time out of mind, a light burning in a window has been recognized as a symbol of hospitality. There are many explanations, some ancient, such as the Christian custom of leaving a candle in a window to welcome the Holy Family. Others are more recent, such as the habit of lighting the way for vagrants and other travelers looking for work during the Depression, or leaving a light burning to metaphorically guide traveling family members home.

Whatever the reasons, most of us respond to light, candles, or a fire in the fireplace as an invitation. So, put lights on the exterior of the house, as shown above, and place lamps at a variety of heights throughout each room, especially near the windows, as in the loft at left. Include candles and oil lamps in as many places as practical, and light them often. And if you have a fireplace—gas or wood burning—use it (within community restrictions, of course).

PINE CONE LAMP

Pine trees and pine cones are enduring symbols of nature.

1 Snip out the top ½" (12.7 mm) of the center of the pine cone. Wrap the pine cone in bubble wrap, and clamp it in a workbench or vise with the base of the pine cone facing up. Using a 12"-long (30.48 cm), ½" (12.7 mm) auger bit, drill a hole all the way through the pine cone.

2 Slide a lock washer and a hex nut onto one end of the threaded brass pipe. Insert the pipe up through the center of the lamp base, and add a threaded brass washer. Tighten the nut and the washer until the pipe is steady within the base.

3 Insert the brass pipe into the hole in the pine cone and gently slide the pine cone down to the base. Top the pipe with a threaded brass washer and then a harp; attach a socket cap. Pull the lamp cord through the nipple and into the socket cap. Tie the split ends of the wire in an underwriter's knot, connect them to the lamp socket, and assemble the socket (see page 126 to 127). Add a lamp shade and, if you like, a finial.

Note: The height of the threaded brass pipe should be in proportion to the size of the pine cone. This pine cone is approximately 8" (20.32 cm) tall, so we used an 11" (27.94 cm) threaded brass pipe.

MATERIALS:

- LARGE PINE CONE • BUBBLE WRAP • LAMP BASE • HEX NUT
- LOCK WASHER • FLAT METAL WASHER
- THREADED BRASS WASHERS (2) • BRASS PIPE THREADED AT EACH END
- HARP • SOCKET CAP • LAMP SOCKET
- LAMP CORD • LAMP SHADE

RUST PAINTED MIRROR

Combine simple materials into a mirror that's a clear reflection of your good taste.

1 Cut a 30 × 42" (76.2 cm × 1.07 m) piece of ½" MDF. Mark a 20 × 32" (50.8 × 81.28 cm) rectangle in the center, then drill a ¼" (6.4 mm) hole at each corner. Slip the blade of a jig saw into a hole and cut out the rectangle, leaving a 5" (12.7 cm) frame. Cut two 29 × 41" (73.66 cm × 1.04 m) pieces of ¼" plywood. Cut a 22 × 36" rectangle out of the center of one of the plywood rectangles.

2 Cover one side of the MDF with wallpaper; carefully miter the paper around the inside and outside edges of the frame. Prime and paint the wallpaper. (We used primer, iron paint, and rust activator by Metal Effects.)

3 Run a zigzag bead of glue around the edges of one side of the plywood frame. Center the plywood frame on the back of the MDF frame. Set the mirror into the plywood frame so that its weight rests on the frame's edges. Top this assembly with the final plywood rectangle, and secure the layers with wallboard screws placed every 4" (10.16 cm) around the perimeter. Apply a coat of polyurethane to the entire assembly and let it dry. Add the hanging hardware and wire.

MATERIALS:

- ½" (12.7 MM) MDF • ¼" (6.4 MM) PLYWOOD
- PAINTABLE, TEXTURED WALLPAPER • LATEX PAINT
- MATTE-FINISH POLYURETHANE SPRAY • 22 × 36" (55.88 × 91.44 CM)
- MIRROR • POLYURETHANE GLUE • 1" (2.54 CM) WALLBOARD SCREWS
- HANGING HARDWARE AND PICTURE WIRE

IRON CHANDELIER

Welcome family and friends to your home with the warm glow of this chandelier.

1 *Use a reciprocating saw with a metal-cutting blade to cut the flat iron into five 24" (60.96 cm) pieces and five 16" (40.64 cm) pieces. (Wear heavy gloves and safety glasses.) Mark each 24" piece, 9½" (24.13 cm) from one end. Select bending forms: Any heavy-duty, round objects with solid edges will work. (We used a 10" automobile flywheel, a 6" toilet*

flange, a 2" pipe flange, and a piece of 1" threaded pipe.) Attach the forms to 2 × 6 (5.08 × 15.24 cm) scraps that can be clamped into a workbench or bench vise.

2 *For each 16" piece, clamp the iron to the 10" form, and shape the entire length of the piece. Lightly tap the iron with a hammer, if necessary, to get it to conform. Remove the iron*

MATERIALS:

- 10" (25.4 CM), 6" (15.24 CM), 2" (5.08 CM), AND 1" (2.54 CM) BENDING FORMS
- 3⅛ × ¾ × 72" (7.9 CM × 19.1 MM × 1.83 M) FLAT IRON BARS • HEAVY GLOVES
- SAFETY GLASSES • 2" (5.08 CM) THREADED BLACK PIPE COUPLERS (2)
- ½" (12.7 MM) × 10-32 PANHEAD MACHINE SCREWS AND NUTS (15 EACH)
- 2" (5.08 CM) WOODEN TOY WHEELS (4) • 2" (5.08 CM) THREADED NIPPLE
- 2½" (6.35 CM) THREADED NIPPLE • LOCK WASHERS (4)
- THREADED BRASS WASHERS (4) • THREADED BRASS CAPS • FINIAL
- ¾" (19.1 MM) × 10-32 PANHEAD MACHINE SCREWS AND NUTS (5)
- 2½" (6.35 CM) UNFINISHED STEEL BOBESCHES (5)
- BLACK DECOR CHAIN (APPROX. 4 FT. [1.22 M])

from the 10" form, reclamp one end to the 1" form, and shape that end into a tight curve. Repeat at the opposite end. For each 24" piece, clamp the marked end to the 6" bending form; wrap the iron around the form, shaping it just past the mark. Next, clamp that same end to the 2" form, and wrap the iron almost all the way around the form. Unwrap the large curve slightly, refining the scroll into a pleasing shape. To curve the other end

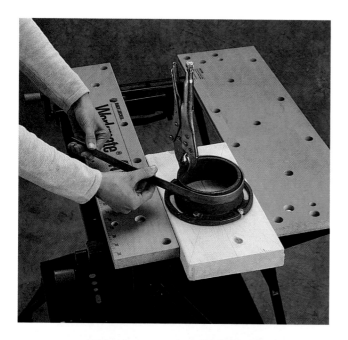

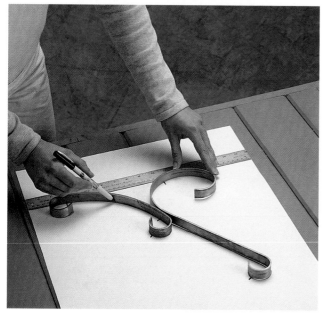

in the opposite direction, turn the piece over and clamp the opposite end to the 2" form; wrap the iron almost all the way around.

◆3 Set a straightedge on a large piece of paper. Lay out one 16" section and one 24" section along the straightedge, and adjust them until they form a pleasing shape. Mark the contact points onto the iron itself, then mark the apex of the large curve on the 24" piece. At each mark, punch and drill a ³⁄₁₆" (4.8 mm) hole. (See Sidebar for information on drilling iron.) Assemble the arm, joining the pieces with ½" machine screws and nuts. Trace the outline onto the paper; use this pattern to arrange and assemble the remaining arms.

◆4 Draw a centerline around the outside of each coupler. Using a square, mark five equidistant points around each coupler, along the centerline. Punch and drill a ³⁄₁₆" hole at each marked point. Attach the arms to the couplers, again using ½" machine screws and nuts. Attach the bobesches to the arms, using ¾" machine screws and nuts.

◆5 Enlarge the center holes in the wooden toy wheels, using a ²⁵⁄₆₄" (9.9 mm) bit. Slide a toy wheel onto the 2" threaded nipple, add a lock washer and a threaded washer, then tighten the threaded washer. Set this assembly inside the lower coupler, resting the toy wheel on the screws and nuts at the center. From beneath the coupler, slide a toy wheel onto the nipple; add a lock washer and a threaded washer, tightening the threaded washer as much as possible. Next, slide a toy wheel onto the 2½" threaded nipple; add a lock washer and a threaded washer and use a pair of pliers to tighten the threaded washer. Add the threaded

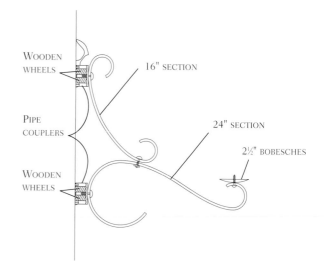

WOODEN WHEELS

16" SECTION

PIPE COUPLERS

24" SECTION

2½" BOBESCHES

WOODEN WHEELS

cap and tighten it by hand. Set this assembly inside the upper coupler, add a toy wheel, a lock washer, and a threaded brass washer. Use a pair of pliers to tighten the threaded washer. Top the stem with a threaded brass washer and a finial. Paint the entire chandelier and let it dry. (We used Metal Effects' iron paint and then added a rust activator.) Clip the chain into the finial, and it's ready to hang.

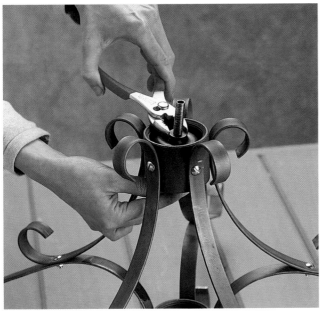

WORKING WITH IRON

When bending strips of cold rolled metal around forms, apply pressure at the first point where the metal meets the form (as shown below). Continue applying pressure in a fluid motion as you work around the form.

The keys to drilling holes in metal are:
• Use high-speed, carbon steel or tempered steel bits.
• Mark the starting point with a centerpunch.
• Keep the tip of the bit well oiled as you drill. A #10 oil, such as sewing machine oil, is best, but any light-weight oil will work.

TECHNIQUES

When Tim and I design projects and describe construction processes, our main goal is to make sure our readers can follow our directions and enjoy the process. We want you to look through this book and think, "I can do that!"

For the most part, the techniques required for these projects are a matter of common sense. Still, we've developed tricks and shortcuts as we've worked with certain materials—twigs and bark for example—that can save you time and aggravation. In the next few pages, you'll find ideas and suggestions on lamp wiring, special paint techniques, and working with twigs and bark.

If a project requires tools or materials you haven't used before, take some time to become familiar with them. If it's possible, practice with scrap materials before you start working on a project—it really will save time in the long run.

If you have questions after reading through the project and techniques, you have a couple of options. First, most hardware stores and home centers have staff members who are happy to answer questions. Many home centers even have classes on the more involved techniques. When you buy materials, ask for help or additional information. If you're still having trouble, call or write to us. You can reach us at Creative Publishing international, 18705 Lake Drive East, Chanhassen, MN 55317 or at DIY@creativepub.com. We love hearing from people who are bringing our ideas to life, and we especially love to see pictures of your creations.

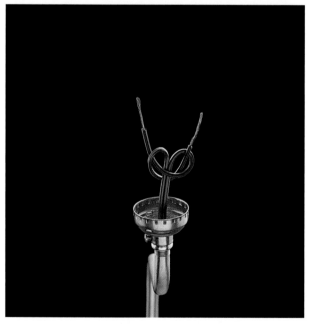

LAMP WIRING

The first time I made a lamp, I was surprised by how easy it was to do the wiring. I guess it seemed mysterious and complicated because I had no idea how few steps it really takes. Basically, all you have to do is thread the lamp cord through the base and up to the socket, and then connect two wires. Very simple—it will probably take less than half an hour to do the whole thing, even the first time. The next time, it will take just a matter of minutes.

Thread the lamp cord through the base and up through the lamp pipe and socket cap. (Many lamp cords are pre-split and the ends are stripped in preparation for wiring. If yours isn't, use a utility knife to split the first 2" [5.08 cm] of the end of the cord, along the midline of the insulation. Strip about ½ to ¾" [12.7 to 19.1 mm] of insulation from the ends of the wires.)

Tie an underwriter's knot by forming an overhand loop

with one wire and an underhand loop with the remaining wire; insert each wire end through the loop of the other wire.

Loosen the terminal screws on the socket. Look carefully at the insulation on the wires—the insulation on one wire will be rounded and on the other wire it will be ribbed or will have a fine line on it. Loop the wire on the rounded side around the socket's brass screw and tighten the screw. Loop the wire on the other side around the socket's silver screw and tighten the screw.

Adjust the underwriter's knot to fit within the base of the socket cap, then position the socket into the socket cap. Slide the insulating sleeve and outer shell over the socket so the terminal screws are fully covered and any slots are correctly aligned.

Test the lamp; when you're sure it works, press the socket assembly down into the socket cap until the socket locks into place.

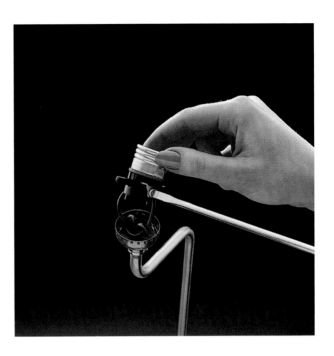

PAINTING

The keys to every good paint job are preparation and patience. This is true whether you're painting the exterior of a house or a tiny bedside table. For these projects, start by lightly sanding the piece, then removing the dust with a tack cloth. Next, apply a coat of primer—sometimes water-based primer and other times pigmented shellac. (The list of materials with each project will guide you.) Let the primer dry, according to the manufacturer's instructions.

The next step in the process is to apply the base coat. Most of the time, this requires two coats. Again, be sure to let the paint dry thoroughly between coats, and add coats until you have a uniform layer of color. When the paint's completely dry, lightly smooth it with fine sandpaper.

For glazing, you can use pre-mixed glaze or combine paint and paint extender in a ratio of 1:1 to create one.

Checkerboard: Glaze the frame and molding, and then the board, as directed on page 92. It's best to add the glaze in layers rather than try to apply too much at one time. To build up layers, let the first coat dry for 48 hours, then repeat.

Cut a piece of tagboard, 18½ × 18½" (47 cm × 47 cm). Draw a 12 × 12" (30.48 cm × 30.48 cm) square, centered on the tagboard (3¼" [8.25 cm] from each edge), then draw a 1½" (3.81 cm) grid within that 12" square. Use a metal straightedge and a razor knife to cut out every other square.

Set the stencil on the board and use a 1" (2.54 cm) brush to apply black glaze to the open squares, moving the brush in the same direction for each stroke. Remove the stencil and let the glaze dry thoroughly. Turn the stencil

180° and paint the remaining squares of the checkboard. Again, add layers of glaze if necessary to make the squares dark enough.

Spatter the entire piece as described below.

Fish Headboard: Prime and paint the headboard. When the paint's completely dry, apply a coat of glaze and let it set for about 5 minutes. Using a damp sponge, strategically remove some of the glaze. Let the base color clearly show through in areas where natural wear patterns would occur, such as the contour of the top and the edges near the posts. (Refer to page 128 for information on building up layers of glaze.)

Take special care when working on the textured areas of the fish. The damp sponge will wick glaze from the surface, and the glaze will naturally seek the recesses. This works just fine, because the point is to emphasize the texture of the fish.

When the glaze is completely dry, add spatters. To do this, dip an old toothbrush in glaze and pat it on paper towels until it's nearly dry. Holding the toothbrush about 3" (7.62 cm) from the surface, slowly scrape your thumbnail across the bristles. Move your hand in a straight line, spattering one area of the headboard at a time. If the speckles are too large, there's too much paint on the toothbrush; pat it on the paper towels again. If they're too fine, you need a little more paint on the brush.

Harvesting fresh wood

If you have wooded areas on your property, you can gather twigs and branches from your own trees. If not, contact builders to see if they'll let you gather wood on property that's scheduled to be cleared. Or visit a brush recycling center. Tim's even been known to stop at commercial construction sites and ask for permission to scavenge through their brush piles. People sometimes laugh, but they rarely refuse.

Many kinds of wood will work for building twig furniture. Often the shape and diameter of the branches are more important than the variety of the tree. For many pieces, it's best to use freshly cut wood—it's easier to work with, and as the wood dries, it shrinks around the nails, which results in sturdier construction.

As you scout for branches, consider the shapes you're trying to create and choose accordingly. Straight pieces are often the best choices, but offshoots and curves will give your pieces dramatic flair. Select branches and twigs that aren't infested with insects, and protect living trees by using sharp cutting tools; ripping or tearing branches could kill small trees.

Harvesting Seasoned wood

Some projects, such as the birch tree table on pages 64 and 65 and the log slice ottoman on pages 78 and 79, require well-seasoned logs. If you're going to cut down a tree, look for one that has been dead for at least one season—the wood should be dry, but not rotten or brittle. If you're harvesting in winter, inspect the tree for new growth buds. If there are no buds, the tree is dead. Keep in mind that most wood-eating insects feed on dead trees. Carefully inspect branches for insects or larvae, and avoid wood from infested trees.

Think about the project you have in mind and, if possible, select one tree that will yield all the material you'll need. The tree should be manageable, however—usually no taller than 25 ft. (7.62 mm).

Cut away the lower branches first. Have someone hold the tree while you cut approximately ¾ of the way through its trunk. Then work together to ease the tree down gently, preserving the upper portions.

If possible, store the harvested wood indoors, to avoid attracting insects. When you're ready to use it, inspect the wood again. If you find tiny holes or other evidence of insects, treat the wood with a safe garden insecticide before beginning your projects.

STRIPPING BIRCH BARK

Choose well-seasoned logs that are at least 4" (10.16 cm) in diameter. Smaller logs are more difficult to strip, they yield less bark, and the bark you do get is cupped and resistant to being reshaped.

Use a straightedge and a utility knife to make a cut along the length of a birch log. Cut all the way through the layers of bark and into the pulp. Starting at one end, use a wide chisel to pry the bark away from the log. When enough bark is loosened, switch to a putty knife or paint scraper, and completely remove the bark from the log. Separate the base layers of the bark from the outer layers to produce a thin, pliable material.

When using the bark, position it to take advantage of its natural shape.

AVERAGE
MANAGEABLE
HEIGHT
25'

1

2

MAKING TWIG FURNITURE

Before you start nailing branches together, drill pilot holes through the top branch and into the bottom one. Use a drill bit that's slightly smaller than the diameter of the nail, such as a ³⁄₃₂" (2.4 mm) bit for 6d (5.08 cm) nails and a ³⁄₆₄" (1.2 mm) bit for 4d (3.81 cm) nails. Make the pilot hole approximately ¾ of the length of the nail you will be using. If you have trouble getting pieces to stay in position while you drill or nail, temporarily lash them together with string or raffia.

Flat-head galvanized nails work well for most joints. The flat heads hold joints firmly; galvanization keeps them from rusting in either green or seasoned wood. The size of nails used depends on the diameter of the branches you're joining. If the nails are too large, they may split the twigs as they dry. Keep an assortment of nails handy as you work. For each joint, select nails that are slightly shorter than the combined thickness of the pieces you're joining.

When a joint is described as a *butt joint*, one piece is to fit flush against the other to form the joint. If *overlap construction* is used, one piece sits over an adjoining piece or pieces to form the joint.

When a project is complete, check all the stretchers, rails, and connecting pieces. Turn the project upside down and try to wiggle the joints. If a joint wobbles at all, drill more pilot holes and add nails until the joint is stable. At a minimum, each joint should have one nail driven straight through both pieces and another at each side, driven at angles (toenailed) into the joint.

After a piece of twig furniture has cured for several weeks, apply exterior wood sealer or a clear acrylic finish. Cover the entire surface of the wood, especially the cut ends of the branches.

Log Cabin Quilt

Fleece Blanket

Linoleum Floor Cloth — enlarge by 800%

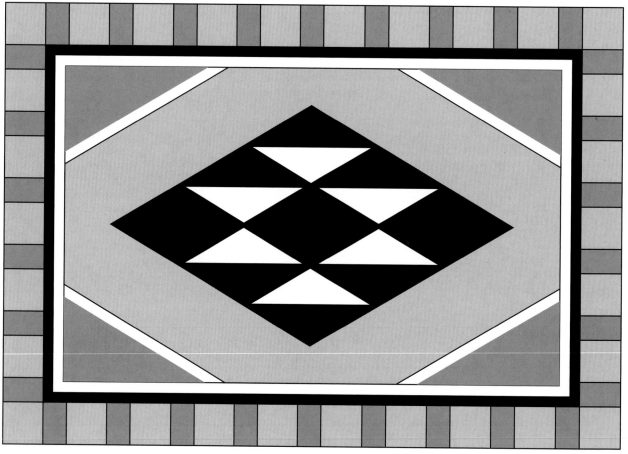

Fleece Blanket Bear —
enlarge by 340%

Fleece Blanket Bear Paw —
enlarge by 145%

Fish Headboard —
enlarge by 225% sm; 350% lg

Fringed Suede Pillow — enlarge by 265%

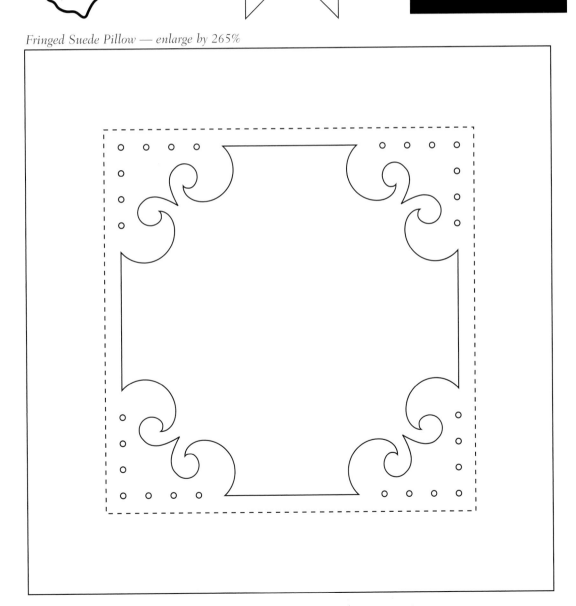

AFTERWORD

Tom Lemmer, a screenwriter I know, once complained to me that his main character was refusing to follow the original story outline. It felt, he said, as though this guy had taken over the plot and simply would not behave. At the time, I thought this was hilarious, but now it makes perfect sense.

As we worked on *Cabin Style*, it took on a life of its own, changing shape and form as if it were an unruly character in one of Tom's stories. In the end, the book became as much about a style of living as it is about a style of decorating. And that's exactly as it should be.

The truth is, no matter how much birch bark or river rock you put into a home, it won't feel like a cabin unless you also create an atmosphere of simplicity and

gracious hospitality. You can hang pictures of wildlife and bend iron bars into chandeliers, but without adding fun to the mix, you will have nothing more (and nothing less) than lovely, well-decorated rooms.

The joy of cabin style is in exploring your own experiences, looking for things that reflect the nameless wildness within you. It is in spinning threads of memories and stories into a cord that connects the past to the future. Perhaps most of all, it is in slowing down, enjoying the beauty and the bounty of nature, and sharing time with friends and family.

I hope you do all those things—and more—as you bring cabin style into your home and into your life.

My best to you and yours,

Jerri

INDEX

INDEX (CONT.)

PHOTOGRAPHERS

Jessie Walker

Glencoe, IL

©Jesse Walker: pp. 6, 11, 12, 13, 18, 21, 22, 23, 24, 26, 27, 28, 29, 31, 32, 33, 34, 35, 42, 44, 46, 57, 59, 60, 63, 71, 72, 77, 88, 89, 101, 102, 112, 113, 136

And for the following:

Susan Chastain, Designer, Chicago, IL: pp. 20, 25, 45, 62, 75, 76, 87, 99, 114;

Chuck Hackley, Designer, Kennilworth, IL: p. 58;

Blacksmith Inn, Wisconsin: p. 100

Karen Melvin

Architectural Stock Images, Inc.

Minneapolis, MN

©Karen Melvin: p.90

And for the following:

Linda Coffey, Designer: pp. 9, 110;

Beth Foss, Associate ASID: p. 10;

Mary Gilbert, Designer: p. 47;

Ard Godfrey House: p. 103;

Larry Hawkins, Designer: p. 61;

Terry Hoffman, Designer: pp. 5, 91;

Trellage-Ferrill Architects & Lighting, Minneapolis, Shawn Trentlage & Darcy Ferrill: pp. 19, 115;

Roddy Turner, Designer: p. 74

CONTRIBUTORS

We would like to thank the following individuals and organizations for their generous support.

Apropolis
1520 East 46th Street
Minneapolis, MN 55407
612-827-1974
rajtarprod@worldnet.att.net

Eddie Bauer Home Store
Mall of America
230 West Market
Bloomington, MN 55425
952-851-0727
www.eddiebauer.com

Smith & Hawken
3464 Galleria
Edina, MN 55435
952-285-1110
www.smithandhawken.com

Sticks & Stones Interiors
4000 Minnetonka Blvd.
Minneapolis, MN 55416
952-926-1567
www.sticks@goldengate.net

Spider Lake Lodge
  Bed & Breakfast Inn
10472 W. Murphy Blvd.
Hayward, WI 54843
Info & Reservations
1-800-OLD-WISC
www.haywardlakes.com/spiderlakelodge

Harmon Interiors – Trude Harmon
780 Como Avenue
St. Paul, MN 55103
651-488-2983

Private collection of Susan & Jim Wolfe
8 Wolfe Lane
South of Forsythe
Forsythe, MT 59327
406-356-7673

From the Collection of Neal Anderson &
  Miriam Buhler
5004 17th Avenue South
Minneapolis, MN 55417
612-729-5913

Dakota Trading Post
Edna Mae Anderson
Alexandria, MN 56308
320-763-3551

Liz Birr
Onahu Log Works
970-669-3004

CREDITS

CREATIVE PUBLISHING international

President/CEO: Michael Eleftheriou
Vice President/Publisher: Linda Ball
Vice President/Retail Sales & Marketing:
  Kevin Haas

Copyright © 2002
Creative Publishing international, Inc.
18705 Lake Drive East
Chanhassen, MN 55317
1-800-328-3895
www.creativepub.com
All rights reserved.

Printed by R.R. Donnelley
10 9 8 7 6 5 4 3 2 1

Library of Congress Cataloging-in-Publication Data

Farris, Jerri.
  Cabin style : ideas & projects for your world / Jerri Farris and Tim Himsel.
    p. cm. -- (Ideas with style)
  Includes bibliographical references and index.
  ISBN 1-58923-058-2 (soft cover)
  1. Rustic woodwork. 2. Country furniture. 3. House furnishings.
  I. Himsel, Tim. II. Title. III. Series.

TT200 .F27 2002
684--dc21
                    2002074152

Executive Editor: Bryan Trandem
Editorial Director: Jerri Farris
Creative Director: Tim Himsel
Managing Editor: Michelle Skudlarek

Authors: Jerri Farris, Tim Himsel
Editor: Barbara Harold
Project Manager: Tracy Stanley
Copy Editor: Tracy Stanley
Assisting Art Director: Russ Kuepper
Mac Designer: Jon Simpson
Stock Photo Editor: Julie Caruso
Technical Photo Stylist: Julie Caruso
Creative Photo Stylist: John Rajtar
Prop Stylist: Paul Gorton
Sample Artist: Sheila Duffy
Director, Production Services & Photography: Kim Gerber
Studio Services Manager: Jeanette Moss McCurdy
Photographers: Tate Carlson, Chuck Nields, Andrea Rugg
Scene Shop Carpenter: Randy Austin
Production Manager: Stasia Dorn
Illustrator: Earl Slack
Author Portraits by: Andrea Rugg
Front Cover Photograph by: Brad Simmons/beateworks.com